WHAT DO ALEXANDER THE GREAT AND BRUCE JENNER HAVE IN COMMON?

Achilles' Heel?

BOTH OF THEM RAN IN OLYMPIC GAMES.

TRACK AND FIELD FACT

TRACK AND FIELD EVEN

BY DAVID PAIGE/CREATIVE

Track and Field

AND STATISTICS ABOUT
S SINCE THE BEGINNING

OUCATION/CHILDRENS PRESS

CONTENTS

The team listed for a player is either the team he was most associated with or the team that he was presently associated with when a particular record was set or a specific event took place.

PHOTO CREDITS

UPI..........cover, 11, 12, 25
Duomo/Bruce Curtis..........6, 14, 18, 21, 22, 28, 30, 31, 34, 39, 41

ILLUSTRATIONS

John Keely..........5, 8, 9, 10, 11

Cover: Early Boston Marathon runners.

Published by Creative Educational Society, Inc., 123 South Broad Street, Mankato, Minnesota 56001. Copyright © 1977 by Creative Educational Society, Inc. International copyrights reserved in all countries. No part of this book may be reproduced in any form without written permission from the publisher. Printed in the United States.

Library of Congress Cataloging in Publication Data
Paige, David.
  Track and field.
  SUMMARY: An illustrated almanac of track and field facts and records such as the first competitor to pole vault eighteen feet and record-holding women hurdlers.
  1. Track-athletics—Records—Juvenile literature. [1. Track and field—Records] I. Title.
GV1060.67.P34   796.4'2'0212   77-173
ISBN 0-87191-606-1

the
sport

Story of Track and Field

The activities of running, jumping, and hurling various objects go back to the earliest days of primitive people. They ran after or away from animals, jumping over things in their path if they had to, and they threw spears and rocks at animals to kill them for food and clothing.

As time went on, people developed competitions to see just who was best at these activities. The first records of people actually competing in track and field events go all the way back to both the Egyptian civilization of approximately 2000 B.C. and to the ancient cultures of China.

In ancient Greece the competition was brought to the level of a sport with the initiation of the Olympics. The following is the story of the evolution of the sport of track and field from that day forward.

777 BC

The first Olympic Games are held in the valley of Olympia, Greece. They consist of only one race, a sprint, which is won by a cook named Coroebus of Elis.

675 BC

Olympic Games are expanded to include other races, field events, a pentathlon (5-event competition), and other sports.

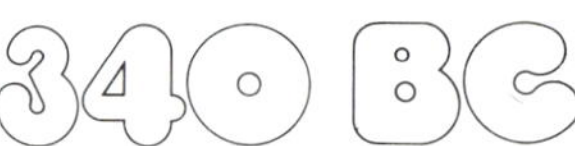

340 BC

Alexander the Great races in the Olympic Games. (He did not win.)

394 AD

The Olympic Games are abolished by Roman Emperor Theodosius.

1154

Track and field outdoor facilities are formally developed in England.

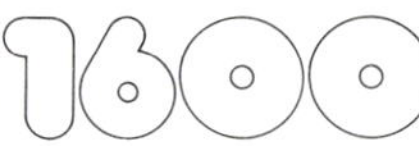

1600

Organized races are held in England. Winners receive awards of money or other items of value.

1862

The first organized track and field meet is held at the Royal Military Academy in Woolwich, England.

1868

The first organized amateur track and field indoor competition to be held in the United States is conducted in New York City by the New York Athletic Club.

1876

The Intercollegiate Association of Amateur Athletes of America (IAAAA) holds its first track and field meet in the United States.

The first U. S. National Amateur championships are held in New York City.

1879

The National Association of Amateur Athletes of America (NAAAA) is established and holds its first national championship track and field meet in New York City.

1880

England's Amateur Athletic Association holds the first track and field championships open to participants from foreign countries.

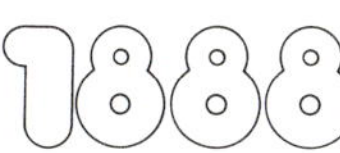

1888

The Amateur Athletic Union (AAU) of the United States conducts its first national championships in Detroit, Michigan.

1890

For the first time, the 100-yard dash is run in less than 10 seconds. John Owen of the United States sprints it in 9.8 seconds.

1895

The Penn Relays are held for the first time at Philadelphia, Pennsylvania, under the auspices of the University of Pennsylvania.

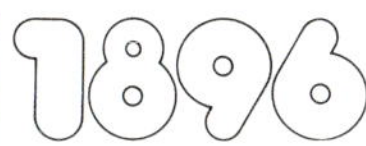

1896

The first modern Olympic Games are held at Athens, Greece. Called Olympiad I, they are the beginning of the modern tradition of international amateur sports competition.

The first Boston Marathon is held in the United States, sponsored by the Boston (Massachusetts) Athletic Association.

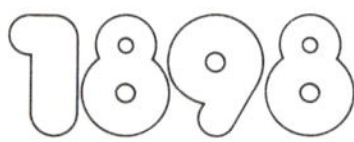

The first international cross-country race is held outside Paris, France. (The distance was slightly more than nine miles.)

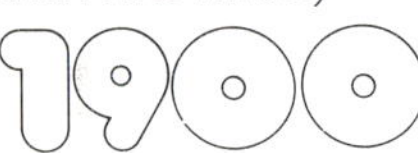

The Olympic Games are held in Paris, France. Among the greats who were winners there: hurdlers J. Walter Tewksbury and Alvin Kraenzlein and hammer throw champ John Flanagan.

The Olympics are held in St. Louis, Missouri. Among the greats: Myer Prinstein, gold medal winner in both the long jump and the triple jump, and discus thrower Martin Sheridan.

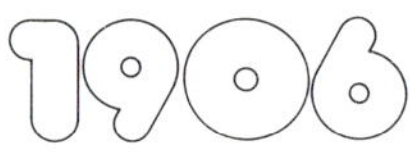

Straying from tradition, the Olympic Games are held in Athens, Greece, only two years after the preceding Olympics. (It is the only time in the history of the Olympics that this occurs.)

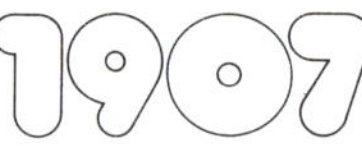

The Millrose Games, a major U. S. national track and field competition, are established in New York City.

The Olympics are held in London, England. Among the greats: Mel Sheppard wins gold medals in both the 800-meter and 1500-meter runs, and Erik Lemming (Sweden) wins the javelin throw.

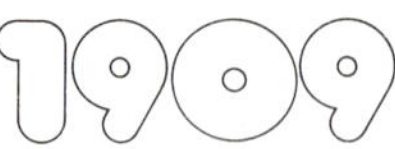

The Drake Relays are instituted at Drake University, Des Moines, Iowa.

The Olympic Games are held at Stockholm, Sweden.

Jim Thorpe wins gold medals and sets Olympic records for both the Pentathlon (5-event competition) and Decathlon (10-event competition). Both medals and records are taken away later when it is found that he had once played in a professional baseball game.

The International Amateur Athletic Federation (IAAF) is established and becomes the governing body for the sport of track and field.

The Olympics are held in Antwerp, Belgium. Paavo Nurmi (Finland) runs in his first Olympics and wins his first gold medal. Charlie Paddock wins the 100-meter sprint.

The National Collegiate Athletic Association (NCAA) holds its first outdoor national championships in track and field.

In Paris, France, the Fédération Sportive Féminine Internationale (FSFI), or International Federation of Sportswomen, is organized to promote and regulate women's competition in track and field.

FSFI conducts the first international track and field championships for women in Paris, France.

The Olympic Games are held in Paris, France. The great distance runner Paavo Nurmi wins four gold medals. Another great is Harold Osborn, who wins a gold medal in both the Decathlon and the high jump.

The Olympics are held in Amsterdam, the Netherlands.

Women are allowed to compete in the Olympics in track and field for the first time.

The Olympic Games are held in Los Angeles, California. Babe Didrikson stars; she is the first woman to win three Olympic medals (two gold, one silver). The great sprinter Eddie Tolan wins gold medals in both the 100-meter and 200-meter sprints.

BABE DIDRIKSON

1936

The Olympics are held in Berlin, Germany. Jesse Owens wins four gold medals and sets three world records. Other greats include Forest Towns, Cornelius Johnson, Earle Meadows, Glenn Morris, and Helen Stephens.

1940

The National Association of Intercollegiate Athletics (NAIA) is founded to promote and govern competition among smaller colleges in the United States. It holds its first national outdoor track and field championships the same year.

1948

After a 12-year lapse due to World War II, the Olympic Games are reinstated at London, England. Fanny Blankers-Koen (Netherlands) becomes the first woman to win four gold medals during a single Olympics. Other greats include: Mel Patton, Mal Whitfield, Harrison Dillard, Bob Mathias, Emil Zatopek (Czechoslovakia), and Micheline Ostermeyer (France).

1952

The Olympics are held in Helsinki, Finland. The great distance runner Emil Zatopek wins three gold medals. Other greats include: Horace Ashenfelter, Andy Stanfield, Bob Richards, Parry O'Brien, and Marjorie Jackson (Australia).

1954

Roger Bannister of England becomes the first person to break the 4-minute mile (3:59.4).

Parry O'Brien of the United States is the first person to hurl the shot more than 60 feet (60–5¼).

1956

Charley Dumas of the United States becomes the first person to high jump seven feet (7–0½).

The Olympic Games are held in Melbourne, Australia. Among the greats: Bobby Morrow, Glenn Davis, Milt Campbell, Al Oerter, and from Australia, Betty Cuthbert and Shirley Strickland.

1960

The Olympics are held in Rome, Italy. Among the greats: Rafer Johnson, Ralph Boston, Abebe Bikila (Ethiopia), Herb Elliott (Australia), Peter Snell (New Zealand), Wilma Rudolph, and Tamara Press (U.S.S.R.).

FANNY BLANKERS-KOEN

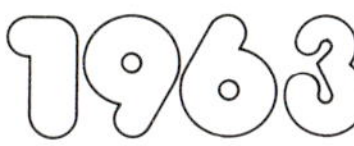

John Pennel of the United States is the first human to pole vault 17 feet (17–0¾).

The NCAA conducts its first national indoor track and field championships.

The Olympic Games are held in Tokyo, Japan. Peter Snell (New Zealand) and Tamara Press (U.S.S.R.) win two gold medals each. Other greats include: Bob Hayes, Valeri Brumel (U.S.S.R.) Mary Rand (England), Wyomia Tyus, and Irina Press (U.S.S.R.).

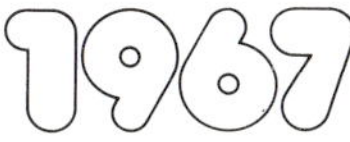

Randy Matson of the United States becomes the first person to shot put more than 70 feet (70–7¼).

Dick Fosbury of the United States introduces a revolutionary form of high jumping that becomes known as the "Fosbury flop."

The Olympics are held in Mexico City, Mexico. Al Oerter wins his fourth consecutive gold medal in the discus throw. Other greats include Kip Keino (Kenya), Tommie Smith, Willie Davenport, Bob Beamon, Bill Toomey, and Wyomia Tyus who wins two more gold medals.

Chris Rapanicolau of Greece becomes the first person to pole vault 18 feet.

The Olympic Games are held in Munich, West Germany. Among the great performers: Frank Shorter, Rod Milburn, Lasse Viren (Finland), Valery Borzov (U.S.S.R.), Mary Peters (England), and Renate Steicher (East Germany).

The Olympics are held at Montreal, Canada. Eight new world records are set, including one for the Decathlon by Bruce Jenner. Other greats include: Alberto Juantorena (Cuba), Edwin Moses, Mac Wilkins, Don Quarrie (Jamaica), Annegret Richter (West Germany), Tatiana Kazankina (U.S.S.R.), and Irena Szewinska (Poland).

men
in
Track & Field

The Sprinters

Event	Record Holder	From	Time (seconds)	Date	Place
60 yards	Herb Washington	U.S.	5.8	Feb. 12, 1972	East Lansing, Michigan
60 meters	Claudiu Suselescu	Rumania	6.4		
	Aleksandr Aksiniw	U.S.S.R.	6.4		
	Alexandr Kornelyuk	U.S.S.R.	6.4		
	Cliff Outlin	U.S.	6.4		
	Juris Silous	U.S.S.R.	6.4		
	Valeri Borzov	U.S.S.R.	6.4		
	Dorel Cristudor	Rumania	6.4		
	Zenon Nowosz	Rumania	6.4		
	Vladimir Oststanov	U.S.S.R.	6.4		
	Erik Gustaffson	Finland	6.4		
	Vassilios Papageorgopolous	Greece	6.4		
	Fyodr Pankratov	U.S.S.R.	6.4		
100 yards	(tie)				
	Houston McTear	U.S.	9.0	May 4, 1975	Long Beach, California
	Ivory Crockett	U.S.	9.0	May 11, 1974	Knoxville, Tennessee
100 meters	Don Quarrie	Jamaica	9.9		
	Harvey Glance	U.S.	9.9		
	Steve Williams	U.S.	9.9		
	Reggie Jones	U.S.	9.9		
	Silvio Leonard	Cuba	9.9		
	Reynaud Robinson	U.S.	9.9		
	Eddie Hart	U.S.	9.9		
	Jim Hines	U.S.	9.9		
	Charlie Greene	U.S.	9.9		
	Ronnie Rae Smith	U.S.	9.9		

The Major Competitions Today

United States	International
AAU Outdoor Championships	The Olympics (every 4 years)
AAU Indoor Championships	The Pan-American Games
NCAA Outdoor Championships	The Asian Games
NCAA Indoor Championships	The Commonwealth Games
Dr. Martin Luther King International Freedom Games	
Millrose Games	
Olympic Invitation Track Meet	
Drake Relays	
Penn Relays	

Sprinters (cont.)

Event	Record Holder	From	Time (seconds)	Date	Place
200 meters (straight track)	Tommie Smith	U.S.	19.5	May 7, 1966	San Jose, California
200 meters (curved track)	(tie) Steve Williams	U.S.	19.8	June 7, 1975	Eugene, Oregon
	Don Quarrie	Jamaica	19.8	June 7, 1975	Eugene, Oregon
	Tommie Smith	U.S.	19.8	Oct. 16, 1968	Mexico City, Mexico
220 Yards (straight track)	Tommie Smith	U.S.	19.5	May 7, 1966	San Jose, California
220 yards (curved track)	(tie) Steve Williams	U.S.	19.9	June 7, 1975	Eugene, Oregon
	Don Quarrie	Jamaica	19.9	June 7, 1975	Eugene, Oregon

Other Great Sprinters

	From	Years of Competition
Charlie Paddock	U.S.	1919–28
Eddie Tolan	U.S.	1928–34
Ralph Metcalfe	U.S.	1928–36
Jesse Owens	U.S.	1930–38
Barney Ewell	U.S.	1938–48
Mel Patton	U.S.	1944–50
Andy Stanfield	U.S.	1948–56
Bobby Morrow	U.S.	1954–58
Bob Hayes	U.S.	1962–64
Hasely Crawford	Trinidad	1974–

The Middle Distance Runners

Event	Record Holder	From	Time (min: sec.)	Date	Place
400 meters	Lee Evans	U.S.	43.86	Oct. 18, 1968	Mexico City, Mexico
440 yards	John Smith	U.S.	44.5	June 26, 1971	Eugene, Oregon
600 yards	Martin McGrady	U.S.	1:07.6	Feb. 27, 1970	New York, New York
800 meters	Alberto Juantorena	Cuba	1:43.5	July 25, 1976	Montreal, Canada
880 yards	Rick Wohlhuter	U.S.	1:44.1	June 8, 1974	Eugene, Oregon
1000 yards	Mark Winzenried	U.S.	2:05.1	Feb. 12, 1972	Louisville, Kentucky
1000 meters	Rick Wohlhuter	U.S.	2:13.9	July 30, 1974	Oslo, Norway

Other Great Middle Distance Runners

	From	Years of Competition
Mel Sheppard	U.S.	1907–12
Arthur Wint	Jamaica	1938–52
Herb McKenley	Jamaica	1944–52
Mal Whitfield	U.S.	1944–54
Charlie Jenkins	U.S.	1954–58
Tom Courtney	U.S.	1954–58
Peter Snell	New Zealand	1958–64
Ralph Doubell	Australia	1965–72
Dave Wottle	U.S.	1970–74

ALBERTO JUANTORENA

The Distance Runners

Event	Record Holder	From	Time (hr: min: sec.)	Date	Place
1500 meters	Filbert Bayi	Tanzania	3:32.2	Feb. 2, 1974	Christchurch, New Zealand
1 mile	John Walker	New Zealand	3:49.4	Aug. 12, 1975	Gothenburg, Sweden
2000 meters	John Walker	New Zealand	4:51.4	June 30, 1976	Oslo, Norway
3000 meters	Brendan Foster	England	7:35.2	Aug. 3, 1974	Gateshead, England
2 miles	Brendan Foster	England	8:13.8	Aug. 27, 1973	London, England
3 miles	Emiel Puttermans	Belgium	12:47.8	Sept. 20, 1972	Brussels, Belgium
5000 meters	Emiel Puttermans	Belgium	13:13.0	Sept. 20, 1972	Brussels, Belgium
6 miles	Ron Clarke	Australia	26:47.0	July 14, 1965	Oslo, Norway
10,000 meters	David Colin Bedford	England	27:30.8	July 13, 1973	London, England
10 miles	Jos Hermens	Netherlands	45:57.0	Oct. 13, 1975	Papendale, Netherlands
20,000 meters	Jos Hermens	Netherlands	57:31.8	Sept. 28, 1975	Papendale, Netherlands
15 miles	Lekka Paivarinta	Finland	1:11:52.6	May 15, 1975	Oulu, Finland
25,000 meters	Lekka Paivarinta	Finland	1:14:16.8	May 15, 1975	Oulu, Finland
30,000 meters	James Alder	England	1:31:39.4	Sept. 5, 1970	London, England

The Marathon

There is not an official Marathon record because the race is run on different courses, each of which has its own peculiarities and degrees of severity.

The official length of the Marathon is 26 miles, 385 yards (42 kilometers).

The following are the fastest times that the Marathon has been run at this distance.

Event	Record Holder	From	Time (hr: min: sec.)	Date	Place
International Marathon	Derek Clayton	Australia	2:08:33.6	May 30, 1969	Antwerp, Belgium
Boston Marathon	Bill Rodgers	U.S.	2:09:55.0	Apr. 21, 1975	Boston, Massachusetts

The Steeplechase

	Record Holder	From	Time (hr: min: sec.)	Date	Place
3000 meters	Anders Garderud	Sweden	8:08.02	July 28, 1976	Montreal, Canada

1976 BOSTON MARATHON

Other Great Distance Runners

	From	Years of Competition
Walter George	England	1878–95
John Paul Jones	U.S.	1908–14
Joie Ray	U.S.	1914–28
Paavo Nurmi	Finland	1918–32
Glenn Cunningham	U.S.	1930–38
Gunder Hagg	Sweden	1938–46
Horace Ashenfelter	U.S.	1944–56
Roger Bannister	England	1950–54
John Landy	Australia	1950–56
Ron Delaney	U.S.	1954–60
Jim Beatty	U.S.	1956–64

	From	Years of Competition
Herb Elliott	Australia	1958–60
Peter Snell	New Zealand	1958–64
Jim Ryun	U.S.	1964–72
Lasse Viren	Finland	1960–

Marathoners

	From	
Emil Zatopek	Czechoslovakia	1944–45
Alain Mimoun	France	1944–66
Abebe Bikila	Ethiopia	1952–64
Kip Keino	Kenya	1960–72
Lasse Viren	Finland	1960–
Frank Shorter	U.S.	1968–

Steeplechasers

	From	
Horace Ashenfelter	U.S.	1944–56
Gaston Roelants	France	1957–68
Kip Keino	Kenya	1960–72

The Hurdlers

High Hurdles (3 feet, 6 inches)

Event	Record Holder	From	Time (seconds)	Date	Place
60 yards	Rod Milburn*	U.S.	6.7	Feb. 12, 1974	Salt Lake City, Utah
	*Professional record				
120 yards	Rod Milburn	U.S.	13.0	June 20, 1973	Eugene, Oregon
110 meters	Guy Drut	France	13.0	Aug. 23, 1975	West Berlin, West Germany

Intermediate Hurdles (3 feet)

Event	Record Holder	From	Time (seconds)	Date	Place
400 meters	Edwin Moses	U.S.	47.6	July 25, 1976	Montreal, Canada

Low Hurdles (2 feet, 6 inches)

Event	Record Holder	From	Time (seconds)	Date	Place
200 meters (straight track)	Don Styron	U.S.	21.9	Apr. 2, 1960	Baton Rouge, Louisiana
200 meters (curved track)	(tie)				
	Glenn Davis	U.S.	22.5	Aug. 20, 1960	Bern, Switzerland
	Karl Lauer	West Germany	22.5	July 7, 1959	Zurich, Switzerland
220 yards	Don Styron	U.S.	21.9	Apr. 2, 1960	Baton Rouge, Louisiana

Other Great Hurdlers

	From	Years of Competition
J. Walter Tewksbury	U.S.	1895–1900
Alvin Kraenzlein	U.S.	1896–1902
Forrest Towns	U.S.	1934–38
Bill Porter	U.S.	1944–50
Harrison Dillard	U.S.	1944–50
Lee Calhoun	U.S.	1953–62
Willie Davenport	U.S.	1962–
Ralph Mann	U.S.	1970–

The Leapers

High Jump

Record Holder	From	Height (ft.–in.)	Date	Place
Dwight Stones	U.S.	7–7.25	August 4, 1976	Philadelphia, Pennsylvania

Other Great High Jumpers

	From	Years of Competition
Harold Osborn	U.S.	1920–28
Cornelius Johnson	U.S.	1931–37
Dave Albritton	U.S.	1934–50
Charley Dumas	U.S.	1954–60
Valery Brumel	U.S.S.R.	1958–62
John Thomas	U.S.	1958–64
Dick Fosbury	U.S.	1966–72

Long Jump

Record Holder	From	Distance (ft.–in.)	Date	Place
Bob Beamon	U.S.	29–2.5	Oct. 18, 1968	Mexico City, Mexico

Other Great Long Jumpers

	From	Years of Competition
James Connolly	U.S.	1896–1906
Bill Hubbard	U.S.	1923–28
Edward Gordon	U.S.	1928–39
Jesse Owens	U.S.	1930–38
Willie Steele	U.S.	1942–48
Ralph Boston	U.S.	1958–68
Arnie Robinson	U.S.	1970–

DWIGHT STONES

Pole Vault

Record Holder	From	Height (ft.–in.)	Date	Place
Dave Roberts	U.S.	18–8.25	June 26, 1976	Eugene, Oregon

Other Great Pole Vaulters

	From	Years of Competition
Earle Meadows	U.S.	1934–44
Cornelius Warmerdam	U.S.	1936–44
Bob Richards	U.S.	1946–56
Don Bragg	U.S.	1955–60
John Pennel	U.S.	1960–72
Wolfgang Nordwig	East Germany	1964–72
Bob Seagren	U.S.	1965–74
Chris Rapanicolau	Greece	1967–74
Steve Smith	U.S.	1971–
Earl Bell	U.S.	1973–

DAVE ROBERTS

Triple Jump (Hop, Step, Jump)

Record Holder	From	Distance (ft.–in.)	Date	Place
Joao Oliveira	Brazil	58–8.25	Oct. 15, 1975	Mexico City, Mexico

Other Great Triple Jumpers

	From	Years of Competition
Myer Prinstein	U.S.	1898–1907
Naoto Tajima	Japan	1932–38
Adhemar da Silva	Brazil	1946–60
Jozef Schmidt	Poland	1956–72
Viktor Saneyev	U.S.S.R.	1965–

The Tossers

Shot Put (16 pounds)

Record Holder	From	Distance (ft.–in.)	Date	Place
Aleksandr Barishnikov	U.S.S.R	72–2.25	July 11, 1976	Paris, France

Other Great Shot Putters

	From	Years of Competition
Al Blozis	U.S.	1940–44
Jim Fuchs	U.S.	1947–53
Parry O'Brien	U.S.	1950–66
Bill Nieder	U.S.	1953–60
Dallas Long	U.S.	1958–64
Randy Matson	U.S.	1963–72
Al Feuerbach	U.S.	1969–
Terry Albritton	U.S.	1973–

Discus Throw (4 pounds, 6.4 ounces)

Record Holder	From	Distance (ft.–in.)	Date	Place
Mac Wilkins	U.S.	232–6	May 1, 1976	San Jose, California

Other Great Discus Throwers

	From	Years of Competition
Martin Sheridan	U.S.	1900–12
Clarence Housner	U.S.	1922–28
Ken Carpenter	U.S.	1932–36
Fortune Gordien	U.S.	1944–71
Al Oerter	U.S.	1955–68
Jay Silvester	U.S.	1966–
John Powell	U.S.	1972–

Hammer Throw

Record Holder	From	Distance (ft.–in.)	Date	Place
Walter Schmidt	West Germany	260–2	Aug. 17, 1975	Frankfurt, West Germany

Other Great Hammer Throwers

	From	Years of Competition
John Flanagan	U.S.	1896–1908
Pat Ryan	U.S.	1916–23
Patrick O'Callaghan	Ireland	1925–38
Anatoly Bondarchuk	U.S.S.R.	1966–74

Javelin Throw

Record Holder	From	Distance (ft.–in.)	Date	Place
Miklos Nemeth	Hungary	310–4.5	July 26, 1976	Montreal, Canada

Other Great Javelin Throwers

	From	Years of Competition
Erik Lemming	Sweden	1900–12
Jonni Myyra	Finland	1912–25
Matti Jarvinen	Finland	1930–38
Bud Held	U.S.	1948–56
Janis Lusis	U.S.S.R.	1968–75
Klaus Wolfermann	West Germany	1971–

SAN JOSE
★ STARS
U.S. OLYMPIC TRIALS
136
EUGENE, OREGON

The Decathlon

A 10-event competition held on two successive days. Scoring is by an internationally accepted point system. The events:

100 meter sprint	Long jump
400 meter run	Pole vault
1500 meter run	Shot put
100 meter hurdles	Discus throw
High jump	Javelin throw

Record Holder	From	Total Points	Date	Place
Bruce Jenner	U.S.	8,618	July 29–30, 1976	Montreal, Canada

Other Great Decathlon Competitors

	From	Years of Competition
Jim Thorpe	U.S.	1908–13
Glenn Morris	U.S.	1934–38
Bob Mathias	U.S.	1948–52
Milt Campbell	U.S.	1952–56
Rafer Johnson	U.S.	1954–60
C. K. Yang	China (Taiwan)	1955–64
Bill Toomey	U.S.	1960–70
Nikolai Avilov	U.S.S.R.	1967–

The Relays

Event	Team Members*	From	Time (min: sec.)	Date	Place
400 meters (100 per man)	Larry Black Bob Taylor Gerry Tinker Eddie Hart	U.S. (all 4)	38.19	Sept. 10, 1972	Munich, West Germany
440 yards (110 per man)	Earl McCulloch Fred Kuller O. J. Simpson Lennox Miller	U.S. U.S. U.S. Jamaica	38.60	June 17, 1967	Provo, Utah
800 meters (200 per man)	Franco Ossala Pasqualino Abeti Luigi Benedetti Pietro Mennea	Italy (all 4)	1:21.5	July 21, 1972	Barletta, Italy
880 yards 220 per man)	Jim Rogers Herbert Woods Marvin Mills Curtis Mills	U.S. (all 4)	1:21.7	Apr. 24, 1970	Des Moines, Iowa
1600 meters (400 per man)	Vince Matthews Ron Freeman Larry James Lee Evans	U.S. (all 4)	2:56.1	Oct. 20, 1968	Mexico City, Mexico
1 mile (440 yards per man)	Lennox Yearwood Kent Bernard Ed Roberts Wendell Mottley	Trinidad & Tobago (all 4)	3:02.8	Aug. 13, 1966	Kingston, Jamaica

*In the order in which they ran.

Event	Team Members*	From	Time (min: sec.)	Date	Place
3200 meters (800 per man)	Manfred Kinder Walter Adams Dieter Bogatzki Franz-Josef Kemper	West Germany (all 4)	7:08.6	Aug. 13, 1966	Wiesbaden, West Germany
2 miles (880 yards per man)	Tom Bach Ken Sparks Lowell Paul Rick Wohlhuter	U.S. (all 4)	7:10.4	May 12, 1973	Durham, North Carolina
6000 meters (1500 per man)	Rod Dixon Anthony Polhill John Walker T. J. Quax	New Zealand (all 4)	14:40.4	Aug. 22, 1973	Oslo, Norway
4 miles (1 mile per man)	Kevin Ross Anthony Polhill Richard Tayler T. J. Quax	New Zealand (all 4)	16:02.8	Feb. 3, 1972	Auckland, New Zealand

*In the order in which they ran.

women
in
Track & Field

The Sprinters

Event	Record Holder	From	Time (seconds)	Date	Place
55 meters	(tie) Angel Doyle	U.S.	6.5	Feb. 7, 1975	Philadelphia, Pennsylvania
	(others) Barbara Terrell	U.S.			
	Rose Allwood	Jamaica			
	Alfreda Daniels	U.S.			
	Mattline Render	U.S.			
	Wyomia Tyus	U.S.			
60 meters	(tie) Andrea Lynch	England	7.2	June 22, 1974	London, England
	(Others) Irina Bochkaryova	U.S.S.R.	7.2	Aug. 28, 1960	Moscow, U.S.S.R.
	Betty Cuthbert	Australia	7.2	Feb. 2, 1960	Sydney, Australia
100 yards	Chi Cheng	China (Taiwan)	10.0	June 13, 1970	Portland, Oregon
100 meters	Annegret Richter	West Germany	11.0	July 25, 1976	Montreal, Canada
200 meters	Renate Stecher	East Germany	22.1	July 21, 1973	Dresden, East Germany
220 yards	Chi Cheng	China (Taiwan)	22.6	July 3, 1970	Los Angeles, California

Other Great Sprinters

	From	Years of Competition
Helen Stephens	U.S.	1934–38
Fanny Blankers-Koen	Netherlands	1946–52
Marjorie Jackson	Australia	1950–58
Wilma Rudolph	U.S.	1956–62
Edith McGuire	U.S.	1962–66
Wyomia Tyus	U.S.	1963–68
Brenda Morehead	U.S.	1973–

ANNEGRET RICHTER (181)

The Middle Distance Runners

Event	Record Holder	From	Time (min: sec.)	Date	Place
400 meters	Irena Szewinska	Poland	49.29	July 29, 1976	Montreal, Canada
440 yards	Irena Szewinska	Poland	51.30	Aug. 29, 1975	London, England
800 meters	Tatiana Kazankina	U.S.S.R.	1:54.94	July 26, 1976	Montreal, Canada
880 yards	Judy Pollock	Australia	2:02.0	June 28, 1967	Helsinki, Finland

Other Great Middle Distance Runners

	From	Years of Competition
Betty Cuthbert	Australia	1955–64
Ann Packer	England	1962–66
Collette Besson	France	1966–71
Kathy Hammond	U.S.	1967–76
Hildegard Falck	West Germany	1968–74
Madeline Jackson	U.S.	1967–
Monika Zehrt	East Germany	1969–

The Distance Runners

Event	Record Holder	From	Time (min: sec.)	Date	Place
1500 meters	Tatiana Kazankina	U.S.S.R.	3:56.0	June 28, 1976	Podolsk, U.S.S.R
1 mile	Paola Cacchi	Italy	4:29.5	Aug. 8, 1973	Viareggio, Italy
3000 meters	Ludmila Bragina	U.S.S.R.	8:27.1	August 7, 1976	College Park, Maryland

The Marathon

There is not an official Marathon record because the race is
run on different courses, each of which has its own
peculiarities and degrees of severity.

The official length of the Marathon is 26 miles, 385 yards.

The following is the fastest time that the Marathon has been
run by a woman at this distance.

Record Holder	From	Time (hr: min: sec.)	Date	Place
Jackie Hansen	U.S.	2:38:19.0	Oct. 12, 1975	Eugene, Oregon

(Because distance races for women are a very recent
competition — the first distance race in the Olympics (1500
meters) was only held in 1972 — there is no formal history of
great female distance runners.)

The Hurdlers

Intermediate Hurdles (3 feet)

Event	Record Holder	From	Time (seconds)	Date	Place
80 meters	V. Korsakova	U.S.S.R.	10.2	June 16, 1968	Riga, U.S.S.R.
100 meters	Annelie Ehrhardt	East Germany	12.3	July 22, 1973	Dresden, East Germany

Low Hurdles (2 feet, 6 inches)

Event	Record Holder	From	Time (seconds)	Date	Place
400 meters	Krystyna Kacperczyk	Poland	56.51	July 13, 1974	Augsburg, West Germany

Other Great Hurdlers

	From	Years of Competition
Babe Didrikson	U.S.	1930–34
Fanny Blankers-Koen	Netherlands	1946–52
Shirley Strickland	Australia	1946–56
Irina Press	U.S.S.R.	1958–65
Chi Cheng	China (Taiwan)	1965–71

The Leapers

High Jump

Record Holder	From	Height (ft.–in.)	Date	Place
Rosemarie Ackerman	East Germany	6–5:25	May 8, 1976	Dresden, East Germany

Other Great High Jumpers

	From	Years Competition
Jean Shiley	U.S.	1928–34
Babe Didrikson	U.S.	1930–34
Alice Coachman	U.S.	1941–48
Mildred McDaniel	U.S.	1953–58
Iolanda Balas	Rumania	1955–64
Ulrike Meyfarth	West Germany	1969–

Long Jump

Record Holder	From	Distance (ft.–in.)	Date	Place
Sigrun Siegl	East Germany	22–11.25	May 19, 1976	Dresden, East Germany

Other Great Long Jumpers

	From	Years of Competition
Elzbieta Krzesinska	Poland	1951–60
Willye White	U.S.	1956–72
Mary Rand	England	1962–68
Heide Rosendahl	West Germany	1966–73
Kathy McMillan	U.S.	1974–

The Tossers

Shot Put (8 pounds, 13 ounces)

Record Holder	From	Distance (ft.–in.)	Date	Place
Helena Fibingerova	Czechoslovakia	72–1.75	Sep. 25, 1976	Opava, Czechoslovakia

Other Great Shot Putters

	From	Years of Competition
Micheline Ostermeyer	France	1945–51
Galina Zybina	U.S.S.R.	1952–64
Earlene Brown	U.S.	1954–64
Tamara Press	U.S.S.R.	1957–65
Nadezhda Chizova	U.S.S.R.	1972–

Javelin Throw

Record Holder	From	Distance (ft.–in.)	Date	Place
Ruth Fuchs	East Germany	226–9.0	July 12, 1976	Berlin, East Germany

Other Great Javelin Throwers

	From	Years of Competition
Babe Didrikson	U.S.	1930–34
Tilly Fleischer	Germany	1932–38
Dana Zatopekova	Czechoslovakia	1952–60
Marjorie Larney	U.S.	1952–60
Kathy Schmidt	U.S.	1968–

Discus Throw (2 pounds, 3 ounces)

Record Holder	From	Distance (ft.–in.)	Date	Place
Faina Melnik	U.S.S.R.	231–3.0	Apr. 24, 1976	Sochi, U.S.S.R.

Other Great Discus Throwers

	From	Years of Competition
Helena Konopacka	Poland	1926–32
Olga Connolly	Czechoslovakia & U.S.	1954–72
Tamara Press	U.S.S.R.	1957–65

The Pentathlon

A 5-event competition held on two successive days. Scoring is by an internationally accepted point system. The events:

200 meter sprint
100 meter hurdles
High jump
Long jump
Shot put

Record Holder	From	Total Points	Date	Place
Burglinde Pollak	East Germany	4,932	Sept. 21–22, 1973	Bonn, West Germany

Other Great Pentathlon Competitors

	From	Years of Competition
Irina Press	U.S.S.R.	1958–65
Mary Peters	England	1970–

The Relays

Event	Team Members*	From	Time (min: sec.)	Date	Place
400 meters (100 per woman)	Doris Maletzki Renate Stecher Christina Heinich Barbel Eckert	East Germany (all 4)	42.51	Aug. 24, 1974	East Berlin, East Germany
440 yards (110 per woman)	Natalya Karnakova Ludmila Maslakova Marina Sidorova Nadyezhda Besfamilnaya	U.S.S.R. (all 4)	44.15	July 5, 1974	Durham, North Carolina
800 meters (200 per woman)	Maureen Tranter Della James Janet Simpson Valerie Peat	England (all 4)	1:33.8	Aug. 24, 1968	London, England
880 yards (220 per woman)	Marian Hoffman Raelene Boyle Pamela Kilborn Jennifer Lamy	Australia (all 4)	1:35.8	Nov. 9, 1969	Brisbane, Australia
1600 meters (400 per woman)	Dagmar Kasling Rita Kuhne Helga Seidler Monika Zehrt	East Germany (all 4)	3:23.0	Sept. 10, 1972	Munich, West Germany
1 mile (440 yards per woman)	Kathy Hammond M. Ferguson Madeline Jackson D. Edwards	U.S.	3:33.9	Aug. 12, 1972	Urbana, Illinois
3200 meters (800 per woman)	Nikolina Chterva Lilyana Tomova Rosita Peckhlivanova Svetla Zlateva	Bulgaria (all 4)	8:05.2	Aug. 30, 1975	Sofia, Bulgaria

*In the order in which they ran.

DAVE ROBERTS SET THE POLE VAULT RECORD OF 18 FEET 8.25 INCHES.
Keep Your Trivia to Yourself!
Jog Out of Here!